DISCOVERING WORLD CULTURES

DISCOVERING WORLD CULTURES

Crabtree Publishing Company

PMB 16A, 350 Fifth Avenue
Suite 3308
New York, NY 10118

612 Welland Avenue
St. Catharines, Ontario
L2M 5V6

Created by McRae Books Srl

Cataloging in Publication Data

MacDonald, Fiona, 1950-
Clothing & jewelry / Fiona MacDonald.
p. cm. -- (Discovering world cultures)
Includes index.
ISBN 0-7787-0236-7 (RLB) -- ISBN 0-7787-0246-4 (pbk.)
1. Costume--History--Juvenile literature. 2.Jewelry--History--Juvenile literature. [1. Clothing and dress. 2. Jewelry.] I. Title: Clothing and jewelry. II. Title. III. Series.
GT518 .M33 2001
391--dc21

00-065993
LC

Coordinating Editor: Ellen Rodger
Production Co-ordinator: Rosie Gowsell
McRae Books Srl
Editors: Holly Willis, Anne McRae
Illustrations: Lorenzo Cecchi, Gian Paolo Faleschini, Antonella Pastorelli, Paola Ravaglia, Studio Stalio (Alessandro Cantucci, Fabiano Fabbrucci, Andrea Morandi, Ivan Stalio)
Design: Marco Nardi, Adriano Nardi, Laura Ottina

Color separations: Litocolor, Florence, Italy
1234567890 Printed and bound in Italy by Nuova G.E.P. 0987654321

CLOTHING *and* JEWELRY

Text by Fiona Macdonald

Illustrations by Antonella Pastorelli, Ivan Stalio, Paola Ravaglia

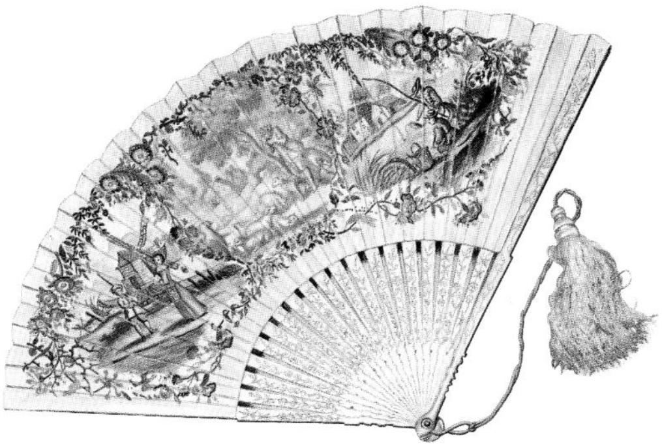

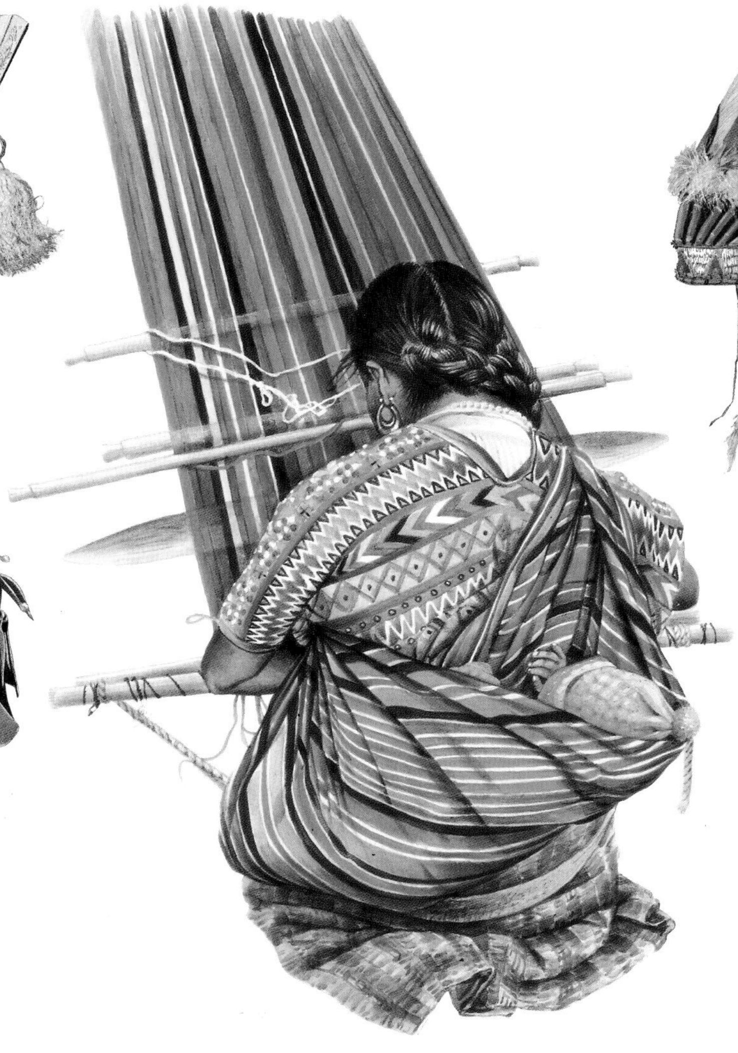

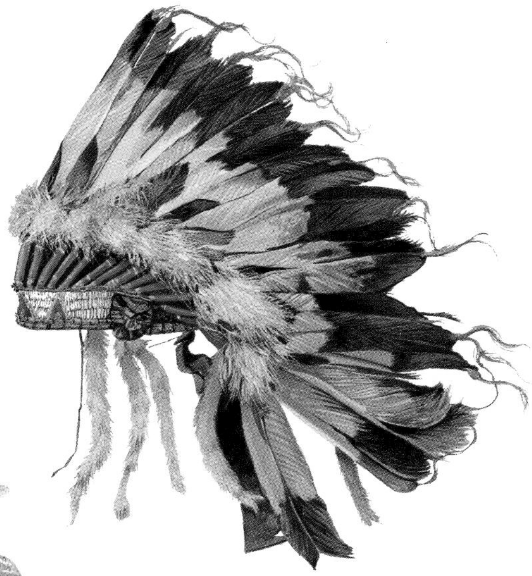

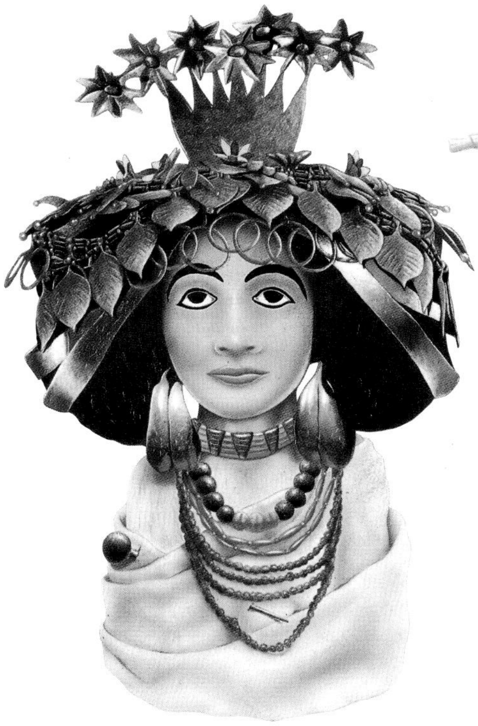

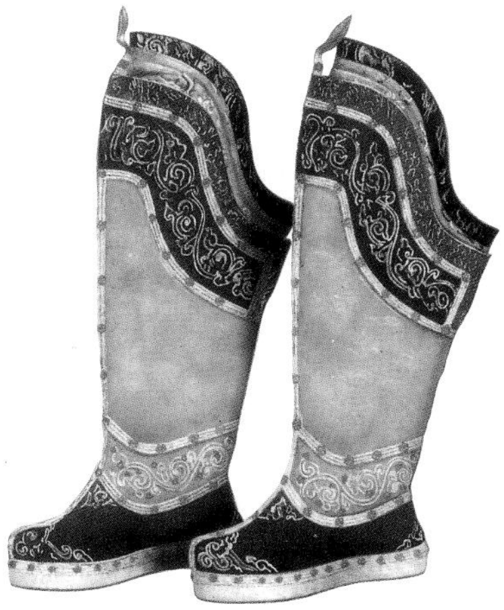

List of Contents

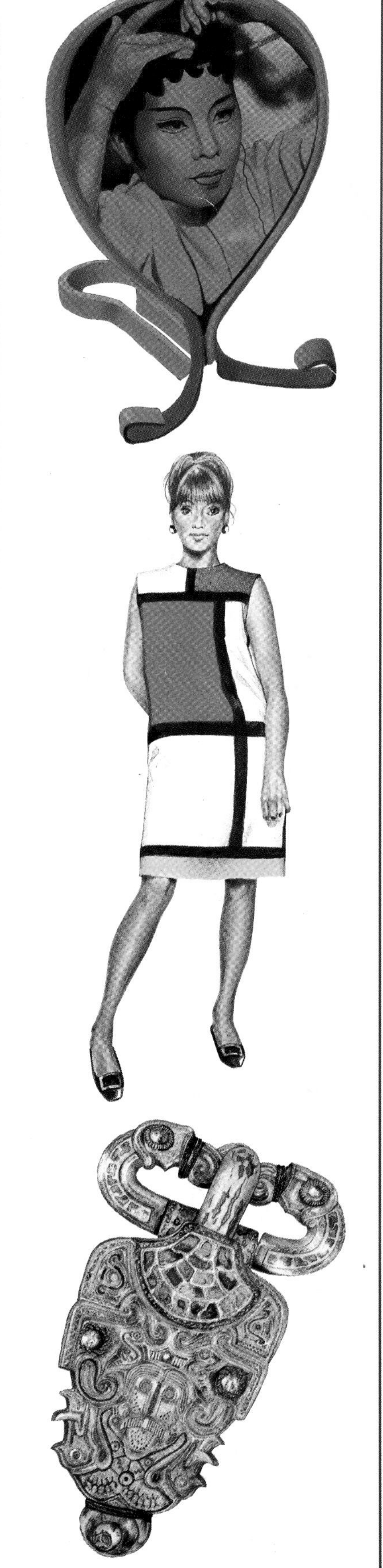

Covering up

In many countries clothing is worn for **modesty**, to cover up naked bodies.

This is a French artist's illustration of mythical people who were thought to have lived in North Africa more than 500 years ago.

Having fun

People everywhere like to dress up in formal clothes or interesting costumes for parties and holidays.

This Italian girl is wearing fresh pasta, called "tagliatelle" on her head and a checkered tablecloth. She is going to a costume party.

What are clothes for?

People wear clothes for many different reasons. In cold climates, they wear them to stay warm and dry. In hot places, they wear light, loose clothing to protect themselves from the burning sun and to keep cool. People with special or dangerous jobs wear uniforms or protective clothing on the job. People also wear clothes to tell others about their position, wealth, and ideas. For example, wealthy and powerful people usually wear clothing that is fancy and expensive, and difficult (or even forbidden) for other people to own. Priests and ministers of many religions wear special robes to show that they belong to a group called the **clergy**.

Fashion

Some people like to dress in the same way as people they admire. The clothes of movie stars, rock singers, or **jet setters** are often copied. The **fashion industry**, based in Paris, Milan, London, and New York, sets new fashions each season. The designers host shows where top models walk down the **catwalks** in the latest styles.

Alexandre Dumas, author of The Three Musketeers, lounges in his fashionable Romantic clothing in 1830.

T-shirts with portraits of Cuban **guerrilla** ***leader Che Guevara were popular with students during the 1960s and 1970s.***

Making statements

People use patterns, designs, pictures, or words on clothing to tell others about their ideas and opinions.

These hand-embroidered silk stockings were high fashion in France during the Romantic period of the late eighteenth/early nineteenth century. Only the rich could afford to be fashionable in the days when clothes were made by hand.

Matadors (below) wear a traditional outfit called a "suit of lights" when they fight the bulls in Spain.

1

Where in the world

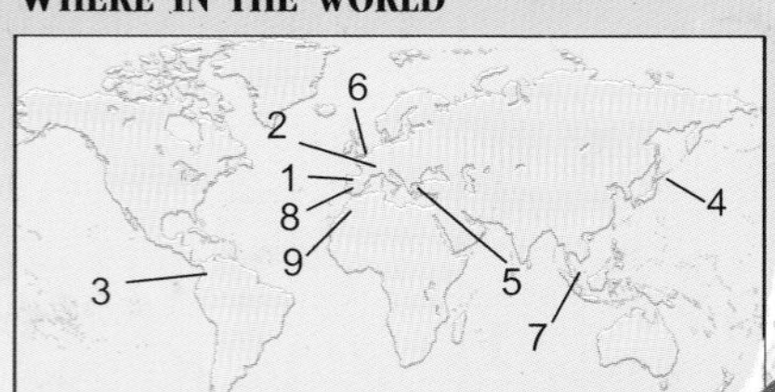

1) Matador (Spain)
2) Breton woman (France)
3) Kogi man (Colombia)
4) Ainu woman (Japan)
5) Ancient Greek statue of a woman (Greece)
6) Anglo-Saxon helmet (England)
7) Kenyah woman (Malaysia)
8) Princess Isabella (Spain)
9) Veiled woman (Morocco)

2

The Breton People

This Roman Catholic woman from Brittany in France is wearing a tall lace cap for the religious pilgrimage she makes each year. The beautiful lace is handwoven by local lacemakers.

The Kogi people

The few remaining Kogi people live in the Andes mountains, in Colombia. The Kogi men weave the cloth to make their simple white clothing. They make just one set and wear it for about 18 months or until it falls apart.

3

The Ainu people

The Ainu people live on Hokkaido, the northernmost island of Japan. Traditionally, they dressed in bark cloth or skins, decorated with geometric designs. The men wore heavy beards and the women had dark blue tattoos around their mouths.

4

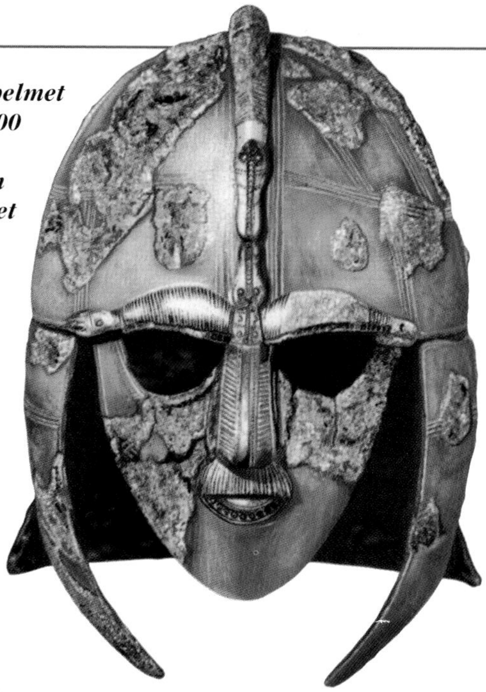

This Anglo-Saxon helmet was made over 1,000 years ago. It was found in a grave in England. The helmet was designed to frighten enemies and protect its wearer in battle.

6

This sixteenth century portrait shows Princess Isabella of Spain. Her luxurious dress is beaded with precious stones and her hat is decorated with pearls and feathers.

Being the boss

Clothing reveals a lot about a person's status or social standing. Wealthy and important people often have very **elaborate** clothing and jewelry. However, the type of clothing varies greatly among different cultures.

8

5

This tiny statue is almost 3,000 years old. It portrays a woman in ancient Greece posing in her beautifully decorated dress. She also wears matching socks.

7

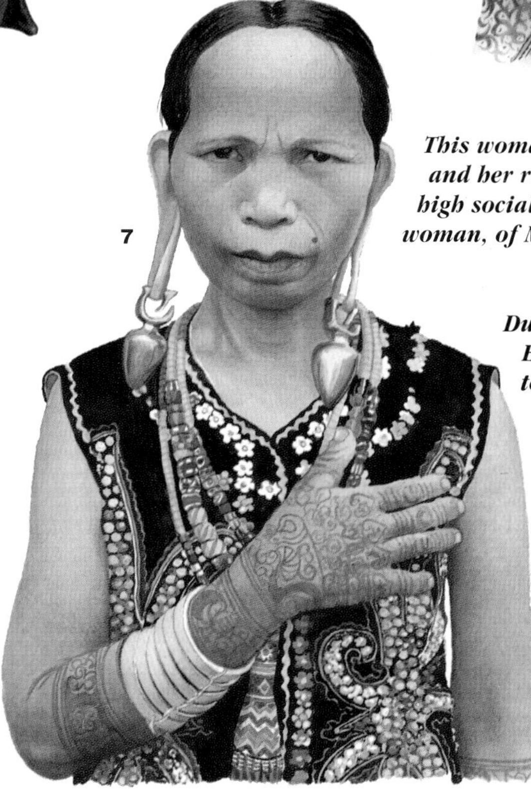

This woman's tattooed arms and hands and her richly beaded vest indicate her high social standing. She is a Kenyah woman, of Malaysia.

During the 1960s, many women in Europe and North America began to dress in more daring clothing, and the miniskirt became fashionable.

Being beautiful

The desire to be attractive encourages men and women to choose clothing with special colors or designs. The type and quality of the material used as well as the design help make a garment more attractive.

9

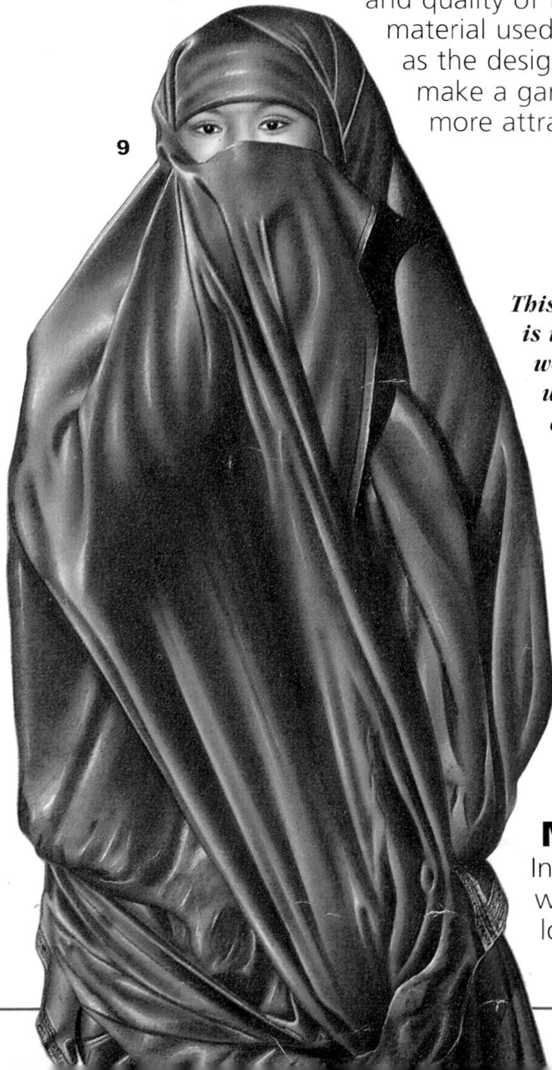

This Moroccan woman is wearing a single length of woolen cloth, called a haik, wrapped around her as a veil and cloak all in one.

American Robert Peary was the first man to reach the North Pole in 1909. The members of his expedition dressed in furs like these as protection against the bitter Arctic cold.

Keeping warm

Clothes can keep out the cold. Without clothing people in cold climates would die. The first clothing, made from animal furs and skins, was probably invented to keep people warm.

Keeping up

Being in fashion is important to some people. It can be an expensive and time-consuming task. Styles change every season and last year's clothing is often discarded even though it still fits.

Modesty

In many Muslim countries, women wear veils and long, loose dresses to cover their body, hair, and face.

Of the past

Old jewelry contains clues about the past. For example, a necklace made with precious stones from many different lands tells us about long-distance trade.

This glass and amber necklace was made by Celts in Europe 2,500 years ago.

About marriage

Married people often wear a ring on the third finger of their left hand. Traditionally, this finger was thought to have a link to the heart.

Many married women in southern India wear a necklace like this "thaali", which reveals details about their family history and their social status.

Jewels speak

The art of making jewelry began in **prehistoric** times when people used materials such as bone, shell, horn and feathers to make body **ornaments**. Many very old cave paintings show people wearing bracelets, rings, and necklaces. People have worn jewelry since ancient times not only to make themselves more attractive, but also to communicate with others. Jewelry can give information about how wealthy the wearer is, whether he or she is married or single, and what religion they follow.

This Chinese silver charm shows the God of Long Life. It was once part of a child's necklace.

To ward off evil

Chinese children wear lucky charms made of silver or brass as protection from evil. These charms are given to a child by friends or family members at a special ceremony held at the end of the first month after birth. The charms are sewn to the child's clothes, or hung round its neck.

In memory of...

Jewels are sometimes made to commemorate a person's life, or the reign of a king or queen.

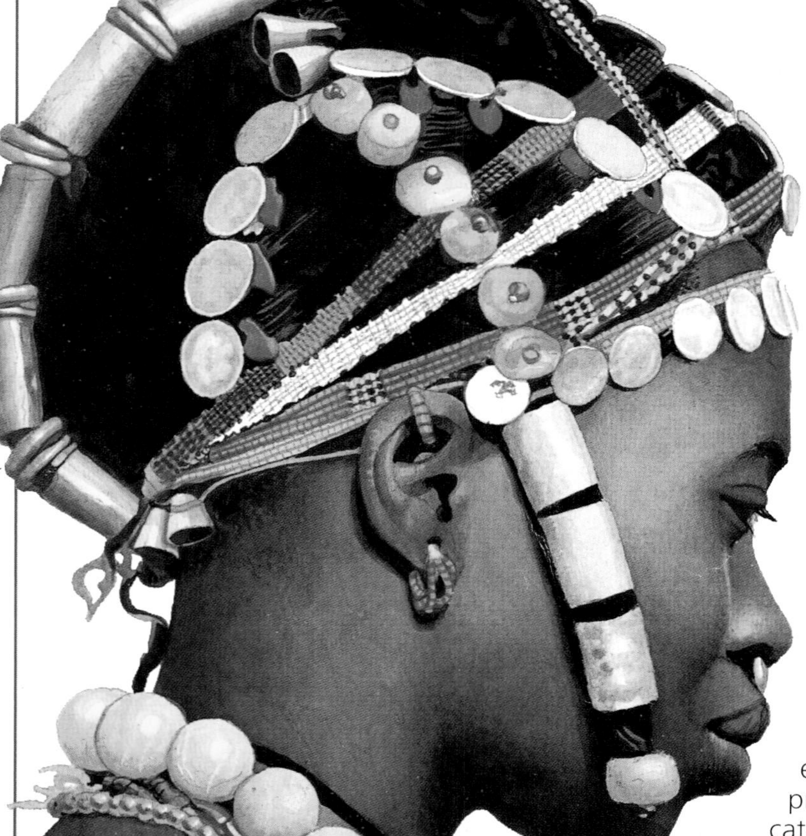

This woman from Mali, in Africa is wearing dramatic jewelry of amber, glass beads, silver, brass, and coins.

Of beauty

People all around the world wear jewelry to look attractive. Jewelry does not have to be expensive or made of precious materials to be eye-catching. Simple things, such as glass beads, shells, or seeds can create a stunning effect.

This cameo, a jewel made from a carved sea shell, portrays the Roman Emperors Claudius and Germanicus, with their wives.

Of change

Jewels are often given as gifts or exchanged to mark important personal moments in our lives, such as growing up or getting married. Such gifts have special meaning and value, for the giver and for the receiver.

This jeweled orb and cross belonged to the Roman Emperors who ruled much of Europe in the Middle Ages.

This African leopardskin belt is decorated with lions' and leopards' teeth. Only chiefs could wear belts like this.

Of wealth and power

Only wealthy and powerful people can afford the most valuable jewelry. It is usually made with costly metals, such as gold, and with precious stones, such as diamonds. Other rare and beautiful objects, such as animal teeth and fur, or brightly-colored feathers, can also be used to create treasures.

Of being young

In South Africa, Zulu men and women wear beaded jewelry. Each bead pattern has a meaning. This belt (right) was made for a young girl, because the figures do not have the tall headdresses that married Zulu women wear.

Among the Tuareg people of North Africa, fathers used to give their sons silver cross-shaped pendants, like this, at puberty.

Of hope and fear

Amulets and charms are worn by people who hope that they will keep away evil spirits and bad luck.

Health and sickness

This necklace belonged to a healer from West Africa. It is made of seeds, beads, **gourds** filled with magic powders, and tiny wooden whistles. The contents of the necklace were believed to cause sickness, death, unhappiness, good luck, riches, or poverty.

This hand-shaped bronze charm was made in ancient Rome. Each magic symbol on the figure guarded the wearer against a different danger.

As a crowning glory

Crowns are worn by kings and queens, or by members of a royal family. They are a sign of royal rank. Often, crowns make the wearer look taller and more important than everyone around them. They are usually decorated with powerful symbols, like the Yoruba bird (right) or the Christian cross (left).

For centuries, St Edward's Crown has been used to crown British kings and queens. Made of gold, it is set with 443 gems.

Tall, beaded crowns, that are almost 16 inches (40 cm) high, were worn by kings of the Yoruba people in West Africa. They were also given as presents to the king's advisors, and to important people visiting the royal court.

Clothing and status

For thousands of years, clothing, jewelry, and hairstyles, have been used to show wealth and power. Kings, queens, and other people of **nobility** wore garments made of the finest fabrics, decorated with jewels to display their wealth. They also wore crowns to show that they were different from ordinary people, and long, flowing robes, as a sign that they did not have to do hard physical work. Plain, simple clothes can also make a statement. They either suggest that the wearer is poor and humble, or that they have more important things to think about than the way they look or what they wear.

Fit for a general

This illustration of a Chinese **warlord** around 1400, shows him wearing a silk robe over armor, a jeweled belt, and embroidered boots. Clothes worn by army leaders were often very detailed. Rich robes and uniforms showed their high rank, and inspired confidence among the soldiers they commanded.

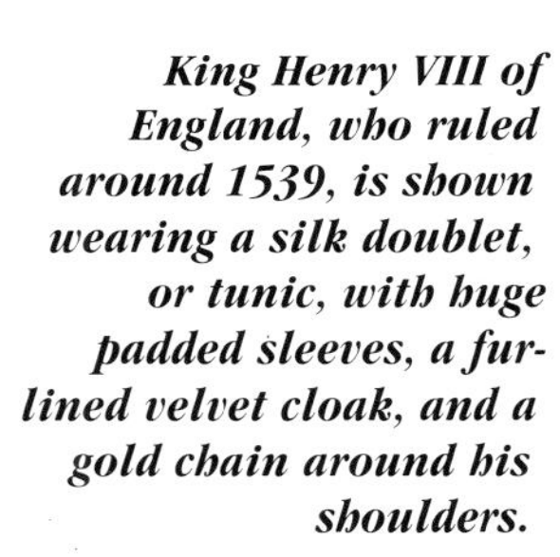

King Henry VIII of England, who ruled around 1539, is shown wearing a silk doublet, or tunic, with huge padded sleeves, a fur-lined velvet cloak, and a gold chain around his shoulders.

Only for a few

In the past, only a few rich or noble people were allowed to own rare and valuable objects. This 'hei tiki' chest pendant was carved in New Zealand from green jade for a Maori nobleman or woman to wear.

Kemal Atatturk became the first president of Turkey in 1923. He wore clothes decorated with gold and silver thread, a wide silk sash, and a jeweled sword at important events.

For political prestige

Kings, queens, and presidents have to look impressive, to create a good image for the nations they rule. Their clothing is often made of rich materials, such as silk or velvet. Leaders and royalty often wear expensive clothing made by famous **designers**.

Decorated in gold

The ancient Egyptians believed that gold was the flesh of the sun-god Ra. He was the special protector of **pharaohs**, who claimed to be **descended** from him. While alive, pharaohs wore rich gold jewelry. After death, their **mummified** bodies were covered with gold funeral masks, and buried in golden coffins.

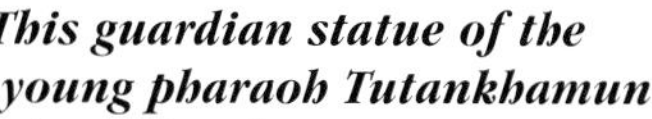

This guardian statue of the young pharaoh Tutankhamun is made of wood with a gilded plaster headdress.

Around 1500, Pope Alexander VI (left) wore a jeweled triple crown, or tiara, and silk cloak to display his wealth and power.

Reveal the power of the spirit

As head of the **Roman Catholic Church**, the pope is a spiritual leader to millions of people. Over the centuries, popes often dressed in different ways, to show their wealth and status. John Paul II chose to wear a simple white robe when he was made pope in 1978. He hoped this would show that he was a humble **Christian**.

For different classes

Until the late twentieth century, people from different **social classes** often dressed in different clothing. This cartoon, from 1920, shows Communist Party leader Vladimir Ilyich Lenin sweeping kings, priests, and factory owners out of Russia. The artist has drawn Lenin wearing a working man's clothing, and his victims wearing crowns, tall hats, and business suits.

The plain, simple robe worn by this Chinese scholar reflects his calm, orderly mind. It shows that he spends his time studying, not thinking about his appearance.

To suit the job

You can often tell a person's occupation from their clothing. Businessmen and women wear neat tailored suits. They dress to look professional. Farmhands and factory workers dress in jeans or overalls. They need clothes that are comfortable and durable.

In high style

Designer fashion has always been very expensive. Only wealthy people can afford to wear the very latest styles created by world-famous designers. This woman from the 1980s is modeling clothes at a fashion show. She is wearing bright red lipstick and a jacket with padded shoulders, which were popular at the time.

This American "freedom suit" was made in 1775 to mark the end of a young man's apprenticeship, or training for a career. It showed that he was qualified, and ready to join the work world.

Is about beauty

This picture of a beautiful woman was painted almost 600 years ago on the walls of a chapel in Florence, Italy. She is shown wearing a hat that was the fashion of her time.

Is ancient

Some fashions are timeless. Although this fresco, or wall-painting, of a goddess from the Roman city of Pompeii is almost 2,000 years old, the loose, flowing style of clothing has often been copied. It became popular around 1800, and again around 1990.

Fashion

Why do we buy new clothes? Over time, old clothing becomes worn out, no longer fits, or is no longer in fashion. In the past, fashions changed slowly and fashionable clothing was expensive. Clothes were made carefully by hand, and news of the latest styles could take years to travel from one country to another. Today, fashions change very fast. Pictures of models wearing the latest styles appear in newspapers, magazines, and on television. Their clothing is copied and quickly appears for sale in stores within weeks. Factory-made clothing and the low wages paid in many clothing factories, mean that fashionable clothes are reasonably priced and more people can now afford them.

Sometimes, clothing designers copy works of art. This 1960s dress was inspired by a painting by modern artist Mondrian.

Can shock

American feminist Amelia Jenks Bloomer was editor of 'The Lily', one of the world's first women's magazines. She campaigned against unhealthy, uncomfortable fashions, such as tight corsets and floor-length skirts. In the 1850s, she and her followers wore comfortable loose pants known as 'bloomers' under knee-length skirts. They were called silly and shocking, and were laughed at in the streets.

Repeats itself?

This ivory figure of a girl (above) seems very modern. It looks like she is wearing sunglasses and a bikini. Looks can be deceiving! Carved almost 6,000 years ago, female figures like this were placed in ancient Egyptian tombs. They were fertility symbols, and helped the dead person's spirit be reborn after death.

Is an art form

Designer clothing, like sculptures, have elegant shapes, and like paintings, can be very colorful. The people who make them are trained, just like other artists. Today's fashion shows are often like rock concerts, with loud music and bright lights.

Trendsetters

Styles chosen by well-known women are often very popular. In the 1960s, Jackie Kennedy, wife of U.S. President John F. Kennedy, was a fashion **trendsetter**. She was famous for her tiny "pillbox" hats and neat, pale-colored suits.

Comes from far away

Many new fashions began out of royal weddings. Wealthy nobles and royalty from other countries would attend these formal events wearing their fanciest clothing. The designs would be copied quickly. Other fashions started when travelers returned from long journeys bringing clothing from distant lands. Wide starched collars, like those worn by this seventeenth-century English nobleman (left) originated in Sri Lanka. They were brought back to the Netherlands by sailors. From there, the fashion spread to France, England, and Spain.

During the late 1960s and 1970s, men and women hippies wore jeans and t-shirts, and grew their hair long.

Was for dolls

In the past, there were no movies, televisions, or magazines to spread pictures of the latest styles around the world. Instead, designers in big cities dressed beautiful dolls in miniature versions of fashionable clothes, and sent them to women living in distant lands. Similar dolls were also sold as toys for rich little girls. This one was made in France to be sent to the Caribbean.

Can be a protest

Many teenagers often wear outrageous clothes, as a way of rebelling against parents and elders. They like the thrill of shocking people and the excitement of creating their own individual style.

Punk fashions spread around the world in the 1980s. This Japanese punk in black leather (above) has short, spiky, bleached hair.

Is different

Ideas about fashion and beauty are different in different parts of the world. Long hair tied in a topknot, and white makeup were considered beautiful in ancient Japan. Japanese women also wore a kimono, a loose robe tied with a silk sash.

Shops like this one (right) are full of fashionable clothes. The style of garments sold will vary from season to season.

Is an industry

Before sewing machines, clothing was made by hand very carefully. Each garment lasted a long time, and fashions changed slowly. Today, fashion is an industry. Fashionable clothes are designed to be worn for just one season. New styles are introduced every year, so that **clothing manufacturers** can sell more, and make more money. Colorful advertisements encourage people to buy the latest fashions.

Shoes with long, pointed toes, called poulaines, were popular in Europe from around 1340 to 1470. Poulaines were worn by men and women, but were mostly popular among teenage boys. Some had points over 23 inches (60 cm) long. The points were stiffened with whalebone, or tied with laces to garters to stop them from flopping.

This marble statue shows a foot in a decorated leather sandal. Found in the city of Alexandria, in Egypt, it is around 2,000 years old and was created as an offering of thanks to a god. Ancient Egyptians prayed to the gods to heal them when they were sick. When they were better, they paid for statues that showed what part of their body had been cured.

Footwear and feet

Shoes and boots have a simple purpose: to keep feet warm, dry, and protected. Shoes are designed to fit the human foot, a part of the body which generally looks the same on people all around the world. Over the centuries, boots, shoes, slippers, and sandals have been made from many different materials in a great variety of shapes and sizes. Footwear is usually sensible and comfortable to wear. Fashionable shoes, however, have often offered little protection from cold or damp, pinching toes and heels. Fashionable footwear is designed to follow the latest trends, and to make the wearer look good.

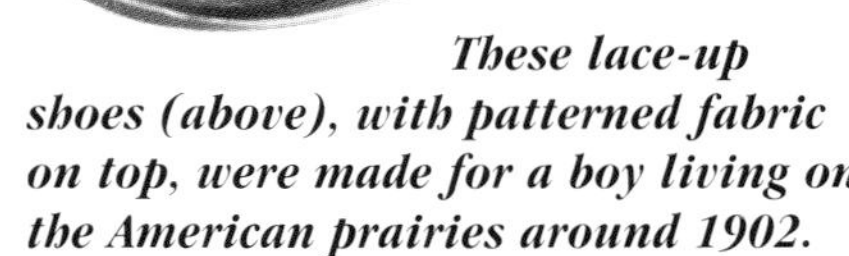

These lace-up shoes (above), with patterned fabric on top, were made for a boy living on the American prairies around 1902.

Footbinding in ancient china

For over 1,000 years, women in high-ranking Chinese families had their feet bound. Tiny feet were a sign of social status, and showed that a woman did not have to work in the fields. They were also believed to be very beautiful. Binding began when a girl was about five years old. Her toes were bent backwards, and tightly bandaged. This prevented her feet from growing normally. Most bound feet were only half the size of fully-grown unbound ones. Special shoes, like these embroidered slippers (below) were made for women with bound feet. Foot-binding was very painful, and left a woman unable to walk normally. It was banned by law in China in 1949.

Boots

Footwear worn on special occasions was often as beautifully decorated as other clothing. These boots, decorated with gold and silk embroidery, were made to be worn by a high-ranking official at the Chinese emperor's court. Their shape is based on the leather riding boots worn by nomadic horsemen who rode across the vast plains of northern China and Mongolia.

Indoor shoes

In Japan it is good manners to remove your outdoor shoes when you enter a house. It is a mark of respect to your hosts. It also prevents the floor from getting muddy or dirty. Traditionally, clean floors were important since Japanese people sat on the floor. Sometimes, visitors were offered slippers to wear or special indoor shoes, like these pretty red sandals.

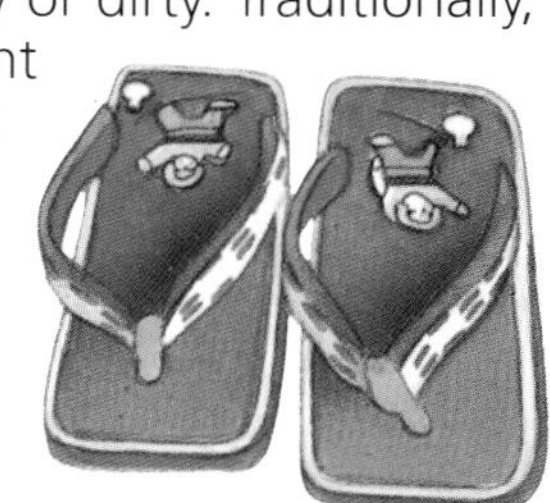

This pair of silk slippers, made for a woman with bound feet, are less than 6 inches (15 cm) long. Compare that with your own shoe size!

Sandals

These ancient Egyptian sandals are made of solid gold. They were not designed to be worn by any living person, but were made to be placed in a tomb, alongside a **mummified** body. The Egyptians believed that people's spirits went on living after death for as long as their body survived. They stocked tombs with everything a spirit might need, from food to furniture and clothes.

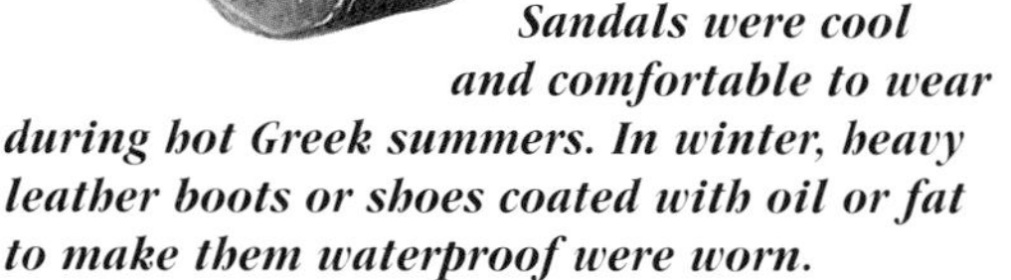

Sandals were cool and comfortable to wear during hot Greek summers. In winter, heavy leather boots or shoes coated with oil or fat to make them waterproof were worn.

A portrait of an English nobleman in 1640 shows him wearing long, soft, tight-fitting boots, topped with a curved, patterned fringe of leather.

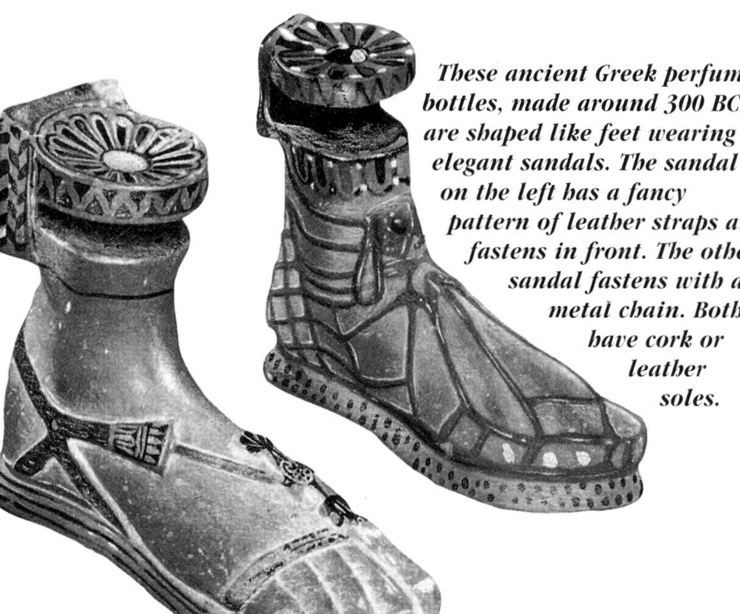

These ancient Greek perfume bottles, made around 300 BC, are shaped like feet wearing elegant sandals. The sandal on the left has a fancy pattern of leather straps and fastens in front. The other sandal fastens with a metal chain. Both have cork or leather soles.

Moccasins were so carefully made that they could probably still be worn even 100 years later!

Moccasins

Native peoples of North America made their clothes and footwear out of the natural materials they found in their environment. These moccasins are made of buckskin, which is the hide of a male deer. Made from a single piece of leather, they are decorated with flowers and leaves using hundreds of tiny beads.

Spy Shoes

This lace-up shoe hides a secret. There is a miniature camera fitted in the heel. The shoe was made around 1940 for a newspaper reporter. He hoped to be able to take photographs without being seen. It must have sometimes been difficult for him to point the camera in the right direction without attracting the attention of a passersby.

These red sequined shoes are magic! They were worn by actress and singer Judy Garland in 1939, in one of Hollywood's most famous films, The Wizard of Oz.

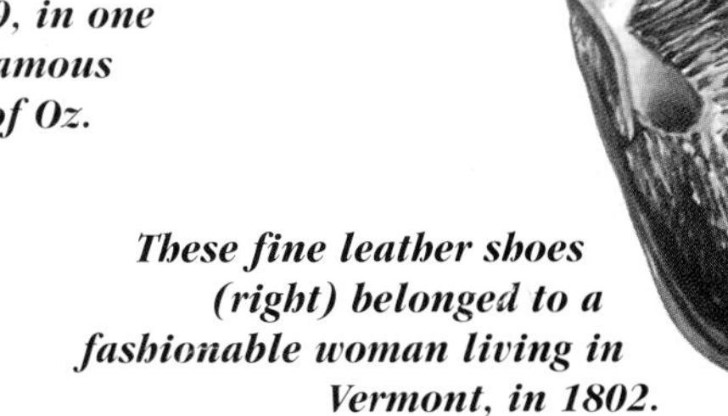

These fine leather shoes (right) belonged to a fashionable woman living in Vermont, in 1802.

A cotton gin was used to separate cotton fibers from the seeds.

Cotton

Cotton is made from the seed pods of a small, bushy plant that grows in warm regions of the world. It was first **cultivated** many thousands of years ago, in India and South America. After processing to remove the sticky seeds, the fluffy cotton fiber can be be spun into a strong thread, suitable for weaving into cloth.

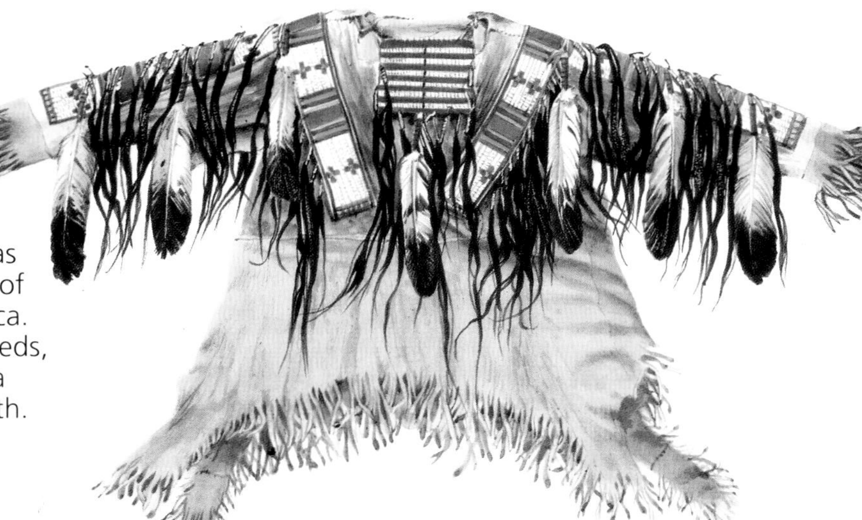

Raw materials

Today, many clothes are made from artificial fibers, such as nylon or polyester. These materials are made in factories from mixtures of **chemicals** such as petroleum or coal. Polyester clothes are strong, tough, and easy to wash and dry. They are also hot and sticky to wear. Before the twentieth century, everyone made clothes from **natural fibers**. Often, people had only a few local materials to choose from, and creating cloth from plants or animal products was a long process. Despite this, many beautiful fabrics were created, such as cool, airy linen or soft, smooth silk, which were pleasant and comfortable to wear.

Skin, beads, and feathers

This deerskin shirt was created around 1896 for a Native American warrior of the Sioux nation. It is decorated with beads and eagle feathers. Deerskin was the usual Sioux material for shirts. Sioux women did not weave cloth

Flax and linen

Flax is one of the oldest plants grown for clothing. Fragments of linen, which is the name for cloth made from flax, have been found in ancient Egyptian tombs and in prehistoric European villages. The flax plant is tall and slender, like grass, with a delicate blue flower. When ripe, flax is cut down, crushed, and left in shallow pools of water, until the outer stalks rot away. This leaves the stringy inner fibers, which are dried and combed before being spun into thread and finally woven into cloth.

Fur and wool

Prehistoric peoples who lived in cold climates needed to wear clothing to keep themselves warm. The soft, thick fur of animals killed for food made warm clothes and blankets. Thinner skins, from smaller animals, could also be turned into clothing. In its raw state, wool from sheep was not useful for making clothing. Once people discovered how to spin and weave, warm, woolen cloth became a favorite fabric. It was lighter and easier to work with than fur, and easier to obtain. Unlike wild animals, sheep did not have to be chased or killed before giving up their wool.

Traditionally, it has been women's work to clean furs and skins and make them into clothes. This Inuit woman from northern Canada is nailing a sealskin to a board, before scraping away the flesh from its inner side with a sharp knife.

These women, pictured on an ancient Greek vase made around 500 BC, are spinning thread and folding finished cloth.

This Mayan woman from Guatemala in Central America is weaving bright cloth using an ancient technique – a back strap loom, invented over 5,000 years ago.

For weaving

In many ancient civilizations, women were expected to produce all the cloth needed to make clothes for their families. This meant spending several hours a day sitting and spinning, or standing and weaving at a tall loom. Many women became expert weavers, and created beautiful patterned clothes for special occasions.

Silk

Silk is the only natural fiber produced by an insect. Silk comes from a special type of moth and has been made in China for almost 10,000 years. To make silk, moth eggs are first hatched into grubs, or worms, called silkworms. When they are fully-grown, they produce strands of fine liquid from glands on their sides. This hardens into silk thread which the worms spin into cocoons. Each silkworm produces about 1640 feet (500 m) of thread. The finished cocoons are then put into boiling water to kill the worms and soften the silk thread. The cocoon can then be carefully unwound, and woven into cloth.

These Chinese women, pictured around 1120, are ironing a newly-woven length of silk. Two hold it stretched tight, while a third presses it with a hot iron.

For coloring cloth

Most natural fibers are usually dull white or pale brown. Clothmakers in many different lands have experimented with **dyes**, such as plant juices and crushed earth, to find ways of coloring cloth. The cloth is boiled for hours in a mixture of dye, water, and a chemical **fixative**, such as alum, or stale urine which 'fixes' the dye to the cloth.

During the Industrial Revolution

Until the 1800s, most cloth was produced at home. Then, during the era known as the Industrial Revolution (1750–1850), engineers invented machines that would spin and weave cloth much more quickly and cheaply than ever before. The water-powered spinning mill was invented by Richard Arkwright, who owned factories in northern England. Around the same time, chemists invented new artificial dyes that were cheap and reliable. The colors they produced were brighter and longer lasting than natural dyes, but many people thought they were ugly.

Heaps of natural dye materials, mostly dried plants, are sold in markets in South America.

To entertain

Actors almost always wear costumes while performing on stage or in front of the camera. They dress up to look like the character they represent, so the audience can better understand the play or the film.

In ancient Greece and Rome, the actors wore comic (happy) or tragic (sad) masks, so the audience sitting at the back of the theater could see their expressions.

This man lives in the Sahara Desert. He is wearing a veil to protect his face from the searing sun and blowing sands.

Dressing up

Special occasions call for special clothing. People like to dress up for parties and special events. Styles and fashions vary greatly from culture to culture, but people everywhere wear special outfits to celebrate a wedding, a birth, or to mourn a death. Some types of clothing are closely linked to certain celebrations. For example, Christian people in Europe traditionally wore new clothes and new hats, known as "Easter Bonnets" on **Easter Day**.

For good luck

This desert-dweller (above) is wearing many amulets, or good luck charms, around his neck, to protect himself and his family against evil spirits.

This ruler from Ghana, in Africa, is wearing a ceremonial robe and gold jewelry. The amulets on his wrists contain verses from the Qur'an, the Muslim holy book.

As an artform

Kimonos are long flowing silk gowns that are traditionally worn by Japanese women on special occasions. Beautiful painted silk kimonos take many months to make by hand. Kimonos are not just clothes, they are also art. They are so valuable that they are handed down from one generation to the next as family heirlooms.

These Japanese women are dressed for a party in colorful silk kimonos. Their hair is worn swept back.

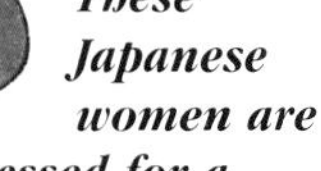

This woman (left) is wearing a French ballgown made in 1949.

To rule a nation

Kings and queens wear **extravagant** clothing on their coronation day, the day when they are publicly proclaimed as the new ruler.

For a night out

People often get dressed up to go to a restaurant, dance, or party.

These Chinese "cat shoes" for babies (above) were decorated with animal faces to scare away evil spirits. The decorated leather cowboy boots (left) were designed for competing in a rodeo.

For a birthday party

Traditionally, Chinese children were given new clothes when they were one month old, and again on their first birthday. Family and friends gathered to celebrate these days with a great feast.

This embroidered satin jacket and pants were given to a one-year-old child in Shanghai, China, in the early 20th century.

For feast days

This diadem, or headdress, from North Africa is made of silver, leather, coral, and monkey fur. It was worn for religious festivals and at weddings.

For Carnival

Carnival is a celebration held before the time of sacrifice and reflection known as Lent. **Lent** is a **Christian** event. In Venice, Italy, people dress up in costumes for Carnival and win prizes for the most original. This man has dressed up as a typewriter!

This mosaic (right) shows the Christian bible story of the Three Kings. The finely dressed kings are taking presents to the baby Jesus

To get married

Marriage is celebrated in hundreds of different ways around the world. It is a happy occasion, when the bride and groom's friends and relatives join together to celebrate the beginnings of a new family.

This bride and groom in Taiwan are dressed in Western wedding clothes. They have already celebrated their marriage according to Buddhist rites.

For eternity

The people of ancient China believed that jade was a magic stone, with special protective powers. They dressed the bodies of important people in jade suits, hoping that they would never decay. This suit of jade squares, fastened together with gold wire, was made for Princess Dou Wan who died around 105 BC. The suit survived, but her body rotted away.

To belong to a group

Mother Teresa (1910–1997) was a **nun** who cared for dying people in India. She founded 'The Order of the Missionaries of Charity', an order of nuns who worked with her. To show that they belonged to Mother Teresa's group, the nuns wore a white **sari** with blue stripes along the border.

Wearing a uniform

People wear uniforms to show that they belong to a group or organization. They wear them to show that they are a member of the same team, go to certain schools, or work in police or fire departments. The uniforms they wear are most often chosen by people in power, such as their employers or the government. Some uniforms are chosen by the wearers themselves. For example, teenagers who all want to wear the same pants, shirts, or shoes as their friends are inventing a uniform all of their own.

To work

Many people, such as doctors in hospitals, dentists, and veterinarians wear long white coats while they are at work. Originally, the coats were designed to protect doctors' clothing from blood, but they also made it easy for everyone to tell who the doctors were.

To save peoples' lives

Firefighters dress in protective clothing, so that they will not get burned by flames or soaked by water from their own hoses. They also wear helmets, to protect their heads from falling beams, thick boots, so their feet will not get burned, and breathing equipment, so that their lungs will not be damaged by smoke and dust.

In the kitchen

Chefs work in hot, steamy kitchens and traditionally wear a white jacket and white, or white checked, pants. To mop up sweat or wipe their fingers, they keep a clean white cloth tucked into their belt, or loosely knotted around their neck. On their heads, they wear a tall white hat, called a "toque." The taller the hat, the more important the chef!

These nurses are dressed in Red Cross uniforms from the First World War (1914–1918).

To guard the emperor

These officers from the **Praetorian Guard** were part of an **elite** corps of 10,000 soldiers that was set up to guard Rome and the emperors who ruled there. On parade, they wore bright red uniforms, and armor decorated in silver and gold.

To go on patrol

Members of the Royal Canadian Mounted Police wear bright red **tunics** and broad-brimmed hats as part of their uniform. In the nineteenth century, the "Mounties" patrolled everywhere on horseback. The style of their uniform dates back to that time.

An army of 6,000 terra cotta, or baked clay, soldiers was buried with Chinese emperor Shi Huangdi after he died in 210 B.C. He hoped they would protect his spirit in the world of the dead.

To do business

Modern businessmen and women feel that it is important to look clean and organized when going to meetings with clients. A neat, well-tailored suit, tidy hair, and polished shoes create a businesslike impression.

To keep evil away

Banners painted with pictures of spirit guardians are displayed outside Chinese houses on New Year's Day. They are meant to protect the family from evil during the coming year, and to bring good luck.

Hold tight!

Buckles and broaches were used for fastening clothes before zippers and buttons were invented. They were often beautiful pieces of jewelry as well. This Viking buckle, dating from around 1000 A.D. is made of gold and silver, and is decorated with an intricate swirling design.

Accessories

Accessories are the belts, jewelry, scarves, and hats that people wear to make their clothing look more fashionable. They are carefully chosen to go with the wearer's clothes, and also to suit their height, weight, and personality. In ancient times, accessories, made of silver and gold, were often used as a way of showing wealth. Today, accessories are used to show the wearer's sense of style and fashion sense.

These black plastic "butterfly" sunglasses (below) decorated with sparkling crystals, were made in Italy in the 1950s. They reflect the glamorous fashions worn by filmstars of that era.

From 4,000 years ago

Incredible jewelry made 4,000 years ago is displayed on this model. **Archeologists** investigating the royal tombs at Ur, a city built by the Sumerian people in the Middle Eastern land known today as Iraq, found the remains of many queens, noblewomen, and royal attendants. The women were dressed in beautiful necklaces, headdresses, and earrings made of gold, silver, and **semi-precious stones**. They had been killed and buried with their dead king.

To see through

For many people, eyeglasses are a necessity. The lenses inside the frames help them see more clearly. They also shade people's eyes from bright light. For most of the twentieth century, glasses have been a fashion accessory, too. Clothing designers and jewelers have produced many decorative eyeglass frames, designed to suit different shaped faces and hairstyles. Eyeglasses first appeared in Europe around 1300, but they may also have been worn in China much earlier.

These solid gold glasses (left) were made in West Africa. They have no lenses in their crisscross patterned frames, and were worn for decoration only.

For everyday use

People in cold climates usually wear gloves in winter to protect their hands from the cold. These thick, padded mittens were made for another purpose. Oven mitts protect hands from being burned while removing hot dishes from an oven. They are made from many different materials, including padded cotton with a fire resistant cover.

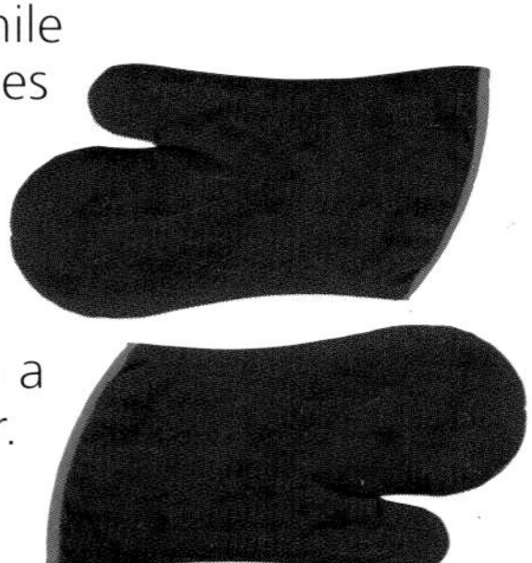

On New Year's Day in Japan, many young girls dress in traditional kimonos, instead of their everyday Western-style clothes. They visit their local Shinto shrine and leave arrows for the gods.

Wrapped in a woolen scarf, this teddy bear (below) is ready to face the winter. Long woolen scarves, or mufflers, were fashionable accessories for men around 1907.

For shelter

These pretty umbrellas and parasols (above) were made in nineteenth century Europe for fashionable women to carry. Their handles were made of wood and metal, their ribs from metal and whalebone. Their covers were made from silk. They were designed to protect the person carrying them. Umbrellas gave shelter from rain. Parasols provided shade from the sun's strong rays. Umbrellas were invented in China during the first century B.C. The first parasols were also made there, about 400 years later.

For men

Many men spend their working lives in business suits made of dark fabric. They are often worn with white shirts. A vivid tie is most men's only chance to display a splash of color with their suits. Belts and suspenders are important fashion accessories, although they are rarely seen. Suspenders are most often worn by older men and young, fashionable businessmen. Belts are worn by almost everyone else!

To aid flirting

Fans were originally invented as a way of circulating cool air. Soon after their invention, they also became tools for flirting. By opening and closing her fan, gently fluttering it, or pretending to hide her face behind it, a woman could send messages to an admirer across a crowded room, without saying a word. The butterfly fan was made in England during the nineteenth century. Its painted gauze wings folded up, like a real butterfly's, by pressing a lever in the handle. The rare, fragile paper fan was also made in England, around 1720. It is decorated with a very delicate print of a country scene, called a mezzotint.

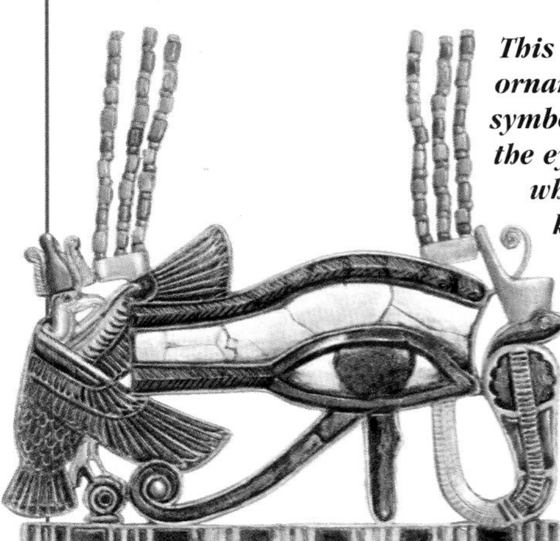

This ancient Egyptian chest ornament shows a magical symbol: the udjet eye, or the eye of the god Horus, who protected Egyptian kings. The ornament was made of gold and lapis lazuli, a semi-precious blue stone. It was found in the tomb of Pharaoh Tutankhamun.

Chassidic apparel

Chassidic **Jews** (pronounced Hassidic) are **ultra-orthodox** and reject many modern ways. Chassidic men wear a full beard, very short hair, and peyot, or side curls. They dress conservatively in black clothing and wear a tallit katan, or prayer shawl. This Chassidic boy lives in New York.

Orthodox robes

Priests of the Orthodox Christian Church, which is based in Russia and Eastern Europe, wear gold embroidered robes to lead church services on festival days. Traditionally, all Orthodox priests have long hair and beards.

Religious Clothes

The clothes people wear can convey their religious or spiritual beliefs. Religious leaders usually wear clothing that identifies them as leaders of a **church**, **mosque**, **temple**, or **synagogue**. Religious worshipers also wear clothing that identifies them as followers of a specific religion. For instance, many **Christians** wear gold crosses as jewelry because the cross is a symbol of **Christ**. Many **Muslim** women follow **hijab**, and wear garments that cover their entire face and body, as a sign of respect, devotion, and faith.

And the Five 'K's

Men who follow the Sikh faith, founded in India in the 15th century by Guru Nanak, show their religion by wearing five outward signs, known as the 'Five Ks'. These signs are kesh, a beard and long hair, covered by a turban; kangha, a comb; kirpan, a short sword; kara, a steel bangle; and kacha, short trousers originally for horse riding.

Holy hairstyles

This girl from Tibet has arranged her hair into 108 braids. This number is sacred to many Tibetan Buddhists. It is thought by some that a person is born with 108 evil desires that they must try to overcome.

These Buddhist priests are chanting hymns at the Moutsuji temple in Japan. They are dressed in purple, a color that is considered sacred or spiritual in many cultures.

For priests

Priests of many religious faiths wear special robes for different times in the year or for special ceremonies. The robes make each festival or service special. Often, the colors of the robes have **symbolic** meaning.

This woman from the Padaung people of northern Thailand (left) is wearing brass rings around her neck to protect her from evil spirits. Some Padaung women wear so many rings that their necks stretch over time and their collarbones and ribs are crushed.

For spiritual power

In Africa, traditional healers and religious leaders have a special place in society. They are respected because they can make contact with the spirits of dead ancestors, who guide and protect living people and guard a family's land. This religious leader from Liberia is dressed in a feathered headdress and fringed robe. The fetishes, or magic charms, strung round his waist help him make contact with ancestor spirits.

For the return of spring

In many northern European countries, traditional festivals celebrate the return of spring. This woman (above) from Estonia is wearing a headdress of fresh green leaves to celebrate a spring festival.

A modern Druid (right) makes his way to a midsummer festival at an ancient holy site in southern Britain. Druids were the priests of the Celtic people, who lived in Europe from around 800 B.C.–100 A.D.

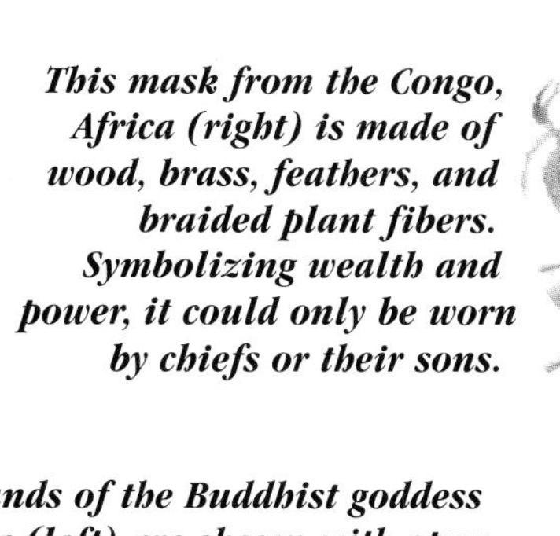

This mask from the Congo, Africa (right) is made of wood, brass, feathers, and braided plant fibers. Symbolizing wealth and power, it could only be worn by chiefs or their sons.

The hands of the Buddhist goddess Tara (left) are shown with open palms facing people who look at her, as a sign that she can grant heavenly help to people in need.

For bejeweled gods

This beautiful statue shows Tara, the Buddhist goddess of **compassion**. The artist who created her has covered her in jewels as a sign of respect. Tara has seven eyes: two eyes on her face, one in the palm of each hand, one in the sole of each foot, and one in her forehead. Buddhists believe that Tara can see everything, and feels pity for all who suffer.

In African masks

There are many different religious customs in Africa, based on ancient traditions in various regions. Masks play an important part in many of them. They are worn by religious leaders or other powerful people during dances, processions and other celebrations, to remind onlookers of unseen spirit powers. Masks may represent the spirits of ancestors, wild animals, or monsters and heroes from myths and legends.

Curls

Long, beautiful curls have often been admired as a sign of youth and beauty. These young women have adorned their curly hair with gold headbands and jewels. They were painted around 1600 B.C. to decorate the royal palace on the Mediterranean island of Crete.

This boy from ancient Egypt is wearing the 'sidelock of youth,' a style for young people only. Most of his head was shaved, but a few strands of hair were left to grow long. They are braided and fastened by a jewelled clasp.

Hairstyles and hats

Hats and hairstyles have both been called "crowning glories". Hats and hair say a lot about a person's lifestyle, religion, and beliefs. People all around the world have invented many different hairstyles, to look well-groomed, or to display their wealth, rank, or religious beliefs. Sometimes people completely covered their hair in wigs or hats, or changed its color with bleaches and dyes. Hairdressing customs became so important that, at various times in the past, going hatless, or wearing long, unkempt hair, was seen as a sign of rebellion.

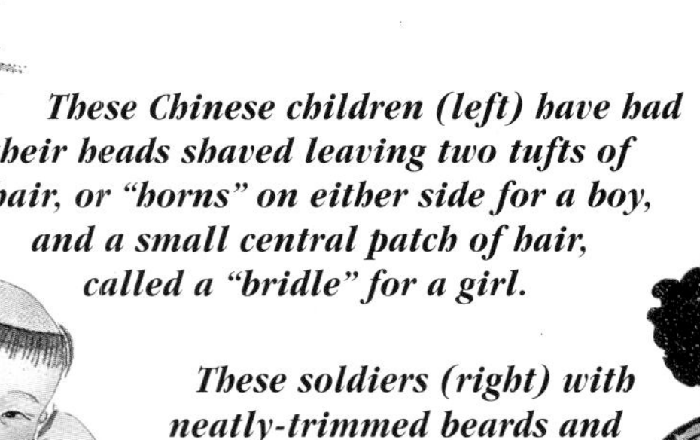

These Chinese children (left) have had their heads shaved leaving two tufts of hair, or "horns" on either side for a boy, and a small central patch of hair, called a "bridle" for a girl.

These soldiers (right) with neatly-trimmed beards and bangs, and shoulder length hair come from ancient Mesopotamia, or present day Iraq, and were painted, almost 4,000 years ago.

Beards

This decorative head (above), made of colored glass, shows a heavily-bearded man from Carthage, a trading city in North Africa that was powerful from around 500–146 B.C. In many countries, men went clean-shaven when they were young and grew a beard as they got older.

Wigs

From 1600 to 1790, almost all wealthy, **nobles** in Europe wore elaborate wigs, made of horse hair padding, sheep's wool, or real human hair. Their own hair was cut very short, so it would not show. Sometimes the wig was powdered white or decorated with flowers, ribbons, or jewels.

This illustration shows Louis XIV wearing a wig in 'full-bottom' style.

Strength

Hair is often thought to be a sign of strength and power. The ancient Chinese believed that someone with thick hair would also have a strong, healthy body. The **Old Testament** story of Samson tells how Samson became weak after his long hair was cut off.

Dreadlocks were first worn by members of the Rastafarian community in Jamaica, in the Caribbean, but have become fashionable among many young people. Rastafarians believe that the Bible forbids them to cut their hair. Growing it "natural" is a sign of devotion and resistance to oppression.

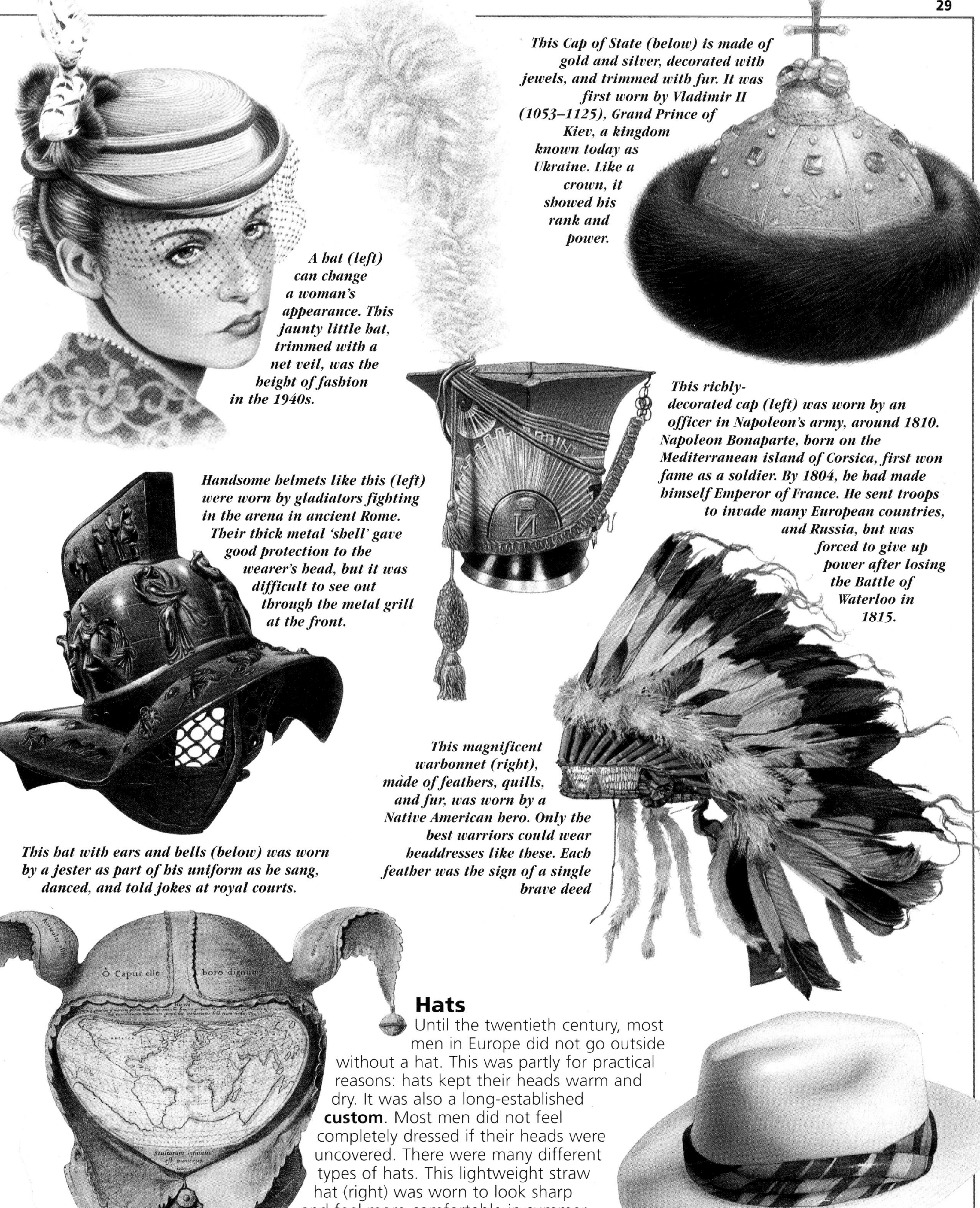

This Cap of State (below) is made of gold and silver, decorated with jewels, and trimmed with fur. It was first worn by Vladimir II (1053–1125), Grand Prince of Kiev, a kingdom known today as Ukraine. Like a crown, it showed his rank and power.

A hat (left) can change a woman's appearance. This jaunty little hat, trimmed with a net veil, was the height of fashion in the 1940s.

This richly-decorated cap (left) was worn by an officer in Napoleon's army, around 1810. Napoleon Bonaparte, born on the Mediterranean island of Corsica, first won fame as a soldier. By 1804, he had made himself Emperor of France. He sent troops to invade many European countries, and Russia, but was forced to give up power after losing the Battle of Waterloo in 1815.

Handsome helmets like this (left) were worn by gladiators fighting in the arena in ancient Rome. Their thick metal 'shell' gave good protection to the wearer's head, but it was difficult to see out through the metal grill at the front.

This magnificent warbonnet (right), made of feathers, quills, and fur, was worn by a Native American hero. Only the best warriors could wear headdresses like these. Each feather was the sign of a single brave deed

This hat with ears and bells (below) was worn by a jester as part of his uniform as he sang, danced, and told jokes at royal courts.

Hats

Until the twentieth century, most men in Europe did not go outside without a hat. This was partly for practical reasons: hats kept their heads warm and dry. It was also a long-established **custom**. Most men did not feel completely dressed if their heads were uncovered. There were many different types of hats. This lightweight straw hat (right) was worn to look sharp and feel more comfortable in summer.

For a sharp smile

Teeth are a part of the body that can be filed down and reshaped. This boy from the Mentawi Islands in Indonesia has had his teeth filed to sharp points. The Mentawi people think that pointed teeth are very attractive.

For going to war

Ancient Celtic warriors from northern Europe who fought against soldiers from **Rome**, went into battle naked. They wore only their weapons and gold torcs, or necklaces. Celtic warriors painted their bodies with a blue plant dye called woad. The woad was thought to give them magical protection from harm.

Body decoration

People have been decorating their bodies for thousands of years. Body paint, tattooing, body piercing, and makeup are still common in many parts of the world. These decorations are believed to make people look more beautiful. They are also worn proudly as badges of achievement, rank, or even **rights of passage**. Sometimes, body decorations can be painful or dangerous. Tattoos can spread infections, for example, and many ingredients used in early makeup were poisonous when absorbed through the skin.

This young girl from the Surma people of Ethiopia has painted her face. Surma men usually paint themselves all over while women paint only their face and chest.

This Aboriginal man from Australia (right) is painting his face with clay and ocher, which is crushed earth. He is taking part in a ceremonial dance. His dancing will retell ancient stories about the Dreamtime, when the ancestors of all living things wandered the earth.

Using special paint

In many warm countries, where people do not wear as many clothes, body painting is a tradition. It makes men and women look attractive to each other and often has a religious meaning as well.

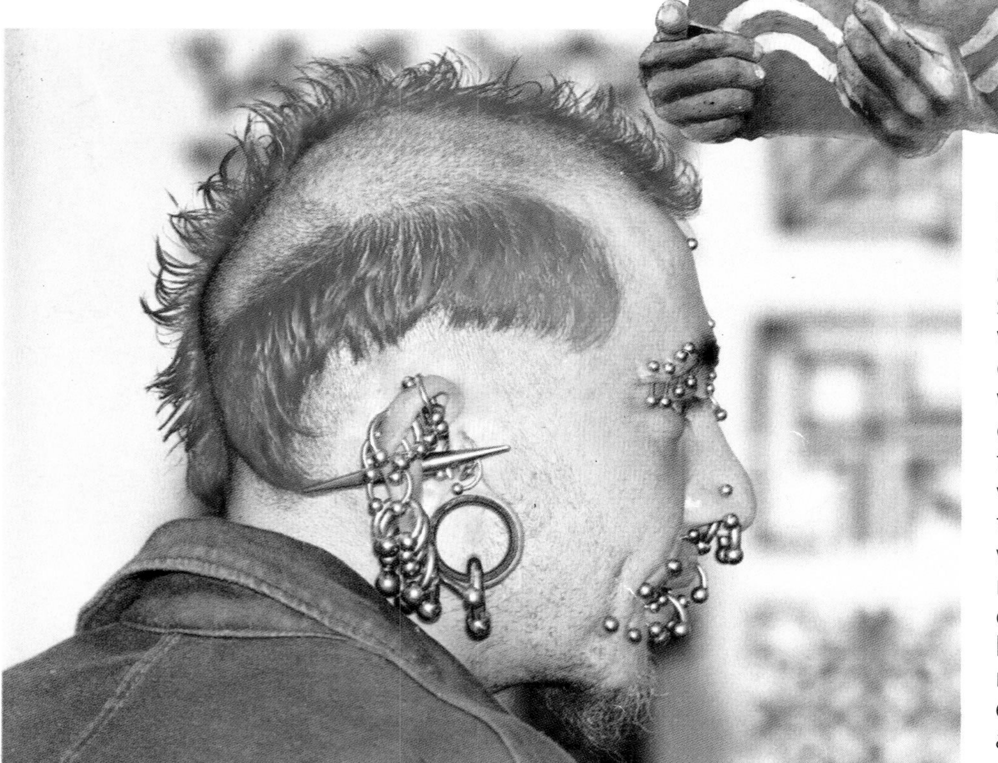

Piercing

Piercing the body and decorating it with metal rings and studs was done in the ancient cultures of Rome and Egypt. It is still popular today. It is common for women, and sometimes men, in many cultures to have their ears pieced and to wear earrings of various shapes, sizes, and colors. Pirates used to wear a gold hoop in their ear so that when they died the valuable earring could be sold to pay for their funeral. Women in India traditionally wear beautiful gold and silver studs in their noses, and this has gradually spread to other countries as well. Body piercing has become fashionable in recent years, and many people have their belly buttons, eyebrows, and even their tongues pierced, although few people have as many piercings as this man (left).

For pretty hands and pretty feet

Hands and feet are some of the most expressive parts of our bodies. They are often on public display in sandals or bare feet, even in countries where people usually keep their bodies covered. In many parts of Africa and Southeast Asia, women and girls decorate their hands with a reddish dye, made from plants called henna. They crush henna leaves to a powder, then mix them with water. The resulting paste is carefully painted in patterns on the skin. The dye lasts for a few days, then fades away. Henna designs are most often worn for weddings.

These beautiful, painted hands (above) belong to a young woman from the Indian Ocean island of Mauritius. Her hands were painted for a performance of the 'dance of love'. The designs are thought to help keep away evil spirits.

Using clever cosmetics

Women and men have used makeup to improve their appearance for thousands of years. Face powder, eyeliner, lipstick, and rouge helped hide scars and blemishes and made them look younger and healthier. The first makeup was made of crushed earth and minerals, sometimes mixed with oil. Plant juices were also used. Some early makeup, such as the white lead powder worn by Roman women, was poisonous and over time, made them very ill.

Marking for life

Tattoos are permanent marks on the skin, made by pricking or scratching the surface and rubbing dye into the wounds to make designs or patterns. Sometimes tattoos are just for decoration. Sometimes they mark a change of status from childhood to adulthood.

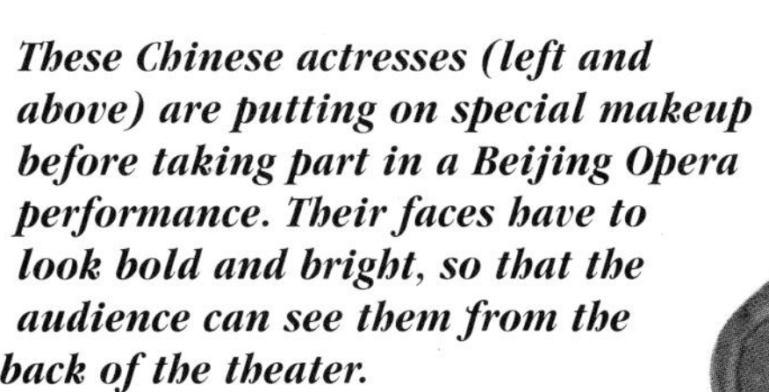

These Chinese actresses (left and above) are putting on special makeup before taking part in a Beijing Opera performance. Their faces have to look bold and bright, so that the audience can see them from the back of the theater.

In male beauty contests

Men from the Wodaabe people of Mali, in West Africa, dress up and paint their faces before taking part in a festival to celebrate the end of the rainy season. There, they parade before unmarried girls, who choose the best-looking men for their husbands.

In Europe

Few people in Europe wear traditional costumes today, except when taking part in folk festivals or performing country dances. Sometimes, people living in popular vacation destinations wear traditional clothes for special events. They believe this helps attract more **tourists**, who spend money in local businesses, take photographs, and buy postcards.

This Dutch woman (left) lives in Marken, Netherlands, a town often visited by tourists. She is wearing the traditional costume of a striped blouse, tight bodice, patterned apron, and a full skirt.

Traditional clothes

Most people today wear very similar clothes. Young people, especially, like to wear the styles they have seen in the movies or on television. In some countries people prefer to wear traditional clothes. Some faiths require men and women to dress modestly for religious reasons. Some people live far away from stores that sell the latest fashions, or they have no money to buy new clothes. Often, people wear traditional clothing as a sign of their personal and national identity, and as an important part of their heritage.

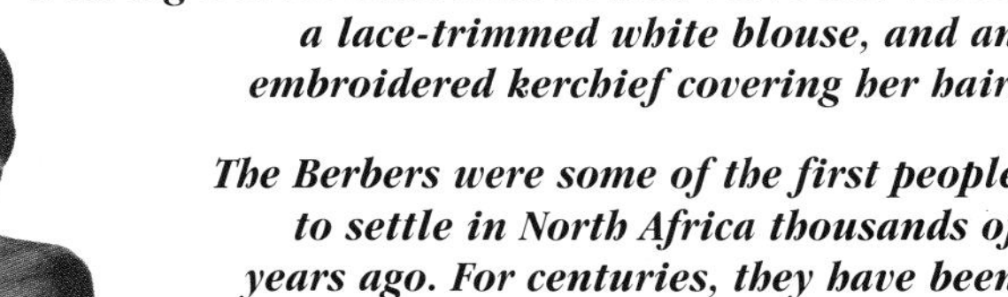

This little girl from Poland is dressed to take part in a festival. She is wearing a dress embroidered with roses and lilies, a lace-trimmed white blouse, and an embroidered kerchief covering her hair.

This young Zulu woman from South Africa wears a headdress (left), that tells us she is married. Its glass bead patterns also have a meaning. They are shaped like shields, and are designed to protect her from attack.

The Berbers were some of the first people to settle in North Africa thousands of years ago. For centuries, they have been famous for their metalworking skills. This Berber bride is wearing traditional heavy, silver jewelry decorated with amber. She will be expected to pass it on to her daughter when she marries.

Men from the Dinka people of Sudan (right) wear tight-fitting leather "corsets" around their waists. Different colors identify different age groups. From 15 to 25, men wear red and black; from 25 to 30, they wear red and purple; over 30, they wear yellow.

In Africa

Africa is a very large continent. It is home to many different peoples, each with their own customs and beliefs. It is not surprising that traditional African clothing comes in many different styles. Like many other ancient, or traditional garments from cultures around the world, each style carries a message about the wearer's age, occupation, wealth, or **marital status.**

In Asia

Many traditional costumes from Asia are very elaborate, and reveal their maker's patience, artistic sense, and skill. Often, they are decorated with items brought from far away. For over 2,000 years, Asia has been at the center of long-distance trade routes, attracting merchants and travelers from many lands.

Akha women (left) from northern Thailand, wear tight, cone-shaped headdresses of dark blue cloth, covered with coins, silver buttons, little mirrors and beads. They are topped by red feather tassels and tufts of monkey fur.

Worn about 150 years ago by a warrior from the Marquesas Islands in the Pacific Ocean, this headband (right) is decorated with a large disk made of turtle shell, mother of pearl, and plant fibers. The Kazakh boy from northwestern China (left) is dressed for a special occasion. He is wearing an embroidered skullcap, waistcoat, white robe, and felt boots.

In North America

Today, most Native Americans wear similar clothes to everyone else in North America. In the past, their clothing was made from animal fur and skins. This nineteenth century woman from the Great Plains region is wearing a shirt, pants, and moccasins of deerskin, as well as a heavy buffalo hide cloak. She has wrapped a woolen blanket, purchased from European traders, around her shoulders.

This young girl (above) from the Kuna people of Panama, in Central America, is wearing a traditional embroidered blouse, heavy silver jewelry, and a red veil.

This boy (above) from the Matse people of the Amazon rainforest, bordering Brazil and Peru, has his face painted like a jaguar. He also has wooden sticks pushed into his skin, to look like jaguar whiskers. The Matse people admire jaguars more than any other animal.

In Latin America

In many countries of Central and South America, Native peoples are in danger. Cattle ranchers, loggers, drug dealers, oil companies, and corrupt politicians have claimed their lands and introduced diseases and alcohol. Native peoples are rarely provided with good education or health care, and are often very poor. Even so, many Native beliefs and traditions have managed to survive. This young couple from Peru have dressed in their best clothes to meet friends on market day.

Hajj

Muslims from all over the world try to make the pilgrimage to a holy place called Mecca once in their lifetime, and this special visit is called Hajj. They go to pray and to visit a building called Ka'bah, that Muslims believe is the first place to have been built for the worship of Allah, or God. Everyone wears special pilgrim clothes before they arrive to help them feel ready to enter a holy place. Men wear two large white cloths, like this boy (left), that they will keep forever. When they die they are buried in them.

Bar Mitzvah

As a sign of respect, people from many different religions wear special clothes when marking festivals or ceremonies. When Jewish boys reach thirteen years of age, their families hold a special ceremony for them called a Bar Mitzvah. It marks the passage from childhood to adulthood. This is the first time Jewish boys read aloud from the Torah, the Jewish holy book, and wear a prayer shawl.

Celebrations and ceremonies

Special events often involve people wearing special clothes. Sometimes people wear their newest or most beautiful clothes to celebrations and ceremonies. In some cultures people wear special costumes to follow a tradition. These costumes are thought to scare away evil spirits. Choosing appropriate clothes for an event is very important. Clothing can show that you have entered a new stage in your life, or that you are carrying out special religious acts.

Chinese New Year

Traditionally, people in many cultures celebrate the New Year with parties and special clothes. Sometimes they dress up, or put on animal masks. These partygoers in China have dressed in lion costumes to scare away evil spirits that might threaten the New Year.

A medieval knighthood

In **medieval Europe**, from 1000 to 1500 A.D., young men from noble families trained to become knights. They served their **lord** or king as fighting men. They followed a strict code of honor and bravery. Men became knights in a special ceremony. First they had a ritual bath, then spent the night in prayer. Finally, they put on a suit of armor, sometimes decorated with **heraldic designs**, and knelt before their lord. He tapped them on the shoulder with his sword. Now they were knights!

Hallowe'en

October 31st is called Hallowe'en. It is the night before All Saints' Day, a day when Christians remember the **saints**. Hallowe'en was influenced by ancient **pagan** beliefs that it was the only night when spirits, ghosts, and witches could wander the earth freely. Today, Hallowe'en is a time when children dress up in costumes and visit people's houses. They say "trick-or-treat," and threaten tricks before being given candy.

At Hallowe'en people hollow out large pumpkins and cut scary faces into them. They put candles inside the pumpkins which give off an eerie glow. These children are about to go "trick-or-treating."

The Sungma Balung Cho Je of the Naxi people (below) wore a silk robe, boots and a cone-shaped hat topped with flags. A glittering metal breastplate covered his chest.

Ceremonial robes for power

Traditionally, the Naxi people of Northwest China asked an oracle, or fortuneteller who could see into the future, for advice. The oracle was called the Sungma Balung Cho Je. The Naxi believed that when he was dressed in a set of magnificent robes, he became possessed by a demon. While **monks** chanted nearby, the demon within him groaned, shook, and spat. Then, the oracle took his bow and arrows and fired into the air to scare away other demons.

Magic

Spiritual leaders often wear special clothing. Their clothing shows that they are different. It sometimes also gives them special magic powers. Traditionally, many tribal people believe that wearing a special costume helps spiritual leaders share in the strength and cunning of certain animals, or makes it possible for them to leave their ordinary bodies and travel in the spirit world.

This carved wood fetish, or magic object from the Congo, in Central Africa, is shaped like a family ancestor. It is decorated with the "life forces" of metal, feathers, and animal skins. It is also hollowed out, and has spaces for special containers of magical objects such as dried animal organs, bones, and herbs.

Glossary

Archaeologist: One who studies objects from past human life and culture found in graves or buildings.

Catwalks: A narrow walkway models walk down during fashion shows.

Chemicals: Artificial and natural substances mixed together to make materials.

Clergy: Priests, ministers, and religious leaders.

Christ: Christians believe he was the son of God.

Christian: Someone who believes in Jesus Christ as the son of God and follows his teachings from the Bible.

Church: A building for public, especially Christian, worship.

Clothing manufacturers: Companies that produce clothing by hand or by machinery, and on a large scale.

Compassion: The awareness of someone's suffering and the desire to help cure it.

Cultivated: Land prepared for growing and tending crops.

Custom: A practice that has been established for a long time, that it has been followed by generations after the time it was created.

Descended: One who has a certain ancestor or ancestry.

Designers: A person who creates new fashion styles for clothing or jewelry, or someone who is creative in some aspect of the arts.

Dyes: A substance used to make color solutions for coloring materials.

Easter Day: The day when Christians celebrate a feast for the resurrection, or rising from death, of Jesus Christ.

Elaborate: To work out in great detail.

Elite: A group or class of people who associate with other people who are intelligent, wealthy, or of high social status.

Extravagant: Spending much more than is needed.

Fashion industry: A business activity involving designer clothes and jewelry.

Fixative: A solution used to protect or preserve something.

Gilded: The addition of gold to give an item a shiny, bright surface.

Gourds: Hard shelled fruit of a gourd plant.

Guerrilla: A member of a group of people organized like soldiers who stage surprise raids on enemy territory.

Heraldic designs: The symbols of a family, or coat of arms. They were often worn on the armor of knights so they could identify enemy soldiers from their own men.

Hijab: The religious rules followed by many Muslims that govern their dress and behavior. Devout Muslim women cover their bodies completely in public when they follow hijab.

Jet setters: A social group of wealthy people who travel from one fashionable place to another.

Jew: A member of a people originally descended from the ancient Hebrews and sharing an ethnic heritage based on Judaism. They believe in one god.

Lent: The period occurring 40 days before Easter, when Christians fast and repent for their sins in preparation for Easter Day.

Lord: A man of high rank. Often someone who owns land that peasants farm.

Marital status: Whether a person is married, unmarried, or divorced.

Medieval Europe: Relating or belonging to the Middle Ages, between the fifth century A.D. and the 1400s.

Modesty: Dressing in a simple manner that is not showy.

Monks: Men who are members of a religious brotherhood. They live in a monastery and are devoted to the discipline of their order.

Mosque: A muslim house of worship.

Mummified: To wrap a dead body into a mummy.

Muslim: A follower of the religion of Islam and the teachings of the Prophet Mohammad.

Natural fibers: Fibers made from original sources, without alteration or artificial changes.

Nobility: A royal, or a person of high rank or class.

Nobles: A group of people recognized by their high rank, class, or social or political status in a country or state.

Nun: A woman who devotes herself to a religious order.

Old Testament: The first of the two main sections of the Christian holy book, the Bible. They correspond to the Hebrew Scriptures.

Ornamented: When items are added to something to make it beautiful to look at.

Ornaments: objects or features used to decorate something.

Pagan: An old term for someone who is not a Christian, Muslim, or Jew.

Pharaoh: An ancient Egyptian king.

Praetorian Guard: The elite bodyguard of an emperor in ancient Rome.

Prehistoric: The time before recorded history.

Priests: A person who has the authority to perform and administer religious rites.

Rights of passage: Events that mark the change from childhood to adulthood.

Roman Catholic Church: The Christian church of which the Pope is the leader.

Rome: A powerful ancient empire. Rome was founded in 753 B.C. It became the center of a vast empire which lasted until 14 A.D.

Saint: A holy person in some religions.

Sari: An outer garment worn by women in India. It consists of one piece of cloth with one end wrapped around the waist to form a skirt and the other draped over the shoulder or covering the head.

Semi-precious stones: Gems that have value but are not as unusual or expensive as precious stones.

Social class: Human society as it is divided into classes according to status.

Symbolic: Something used as a symbol or representation of something else.

Synagogue: A building or place of worship and religious instruction in the Jewish faith.

Temple: A building where religious ceremonies or worship take place.

Trendsetter: A person who establishes a new style or fashion for others.

Tourist: Someone who travels for pleasure

Tunics: A long, plain, close-fitting military jacket, usually with a stiff high collar.

Ultra-orthodox: one who is extremely dedicated to adhering to their accepted, or traditional faith.

Warlord: A military commander who has control of a region in a country.

Index

Acknowledgments

The publishers would like to thank the following picture libraries and photographers for their kind permission to reproduce pictures:

t=top; tl=top left; tc=top center; tr=top right; c=center;
cl=center left; b=bottom; bl=bottom left; bc=bottom center; br=bottom right

Marco Lanza: p 8tr
Anne McRae / McRae Books: p15b
Adriano Nardi / McRae Books: p 21cl
Marco Nardi / McRae Books: p 21b; p 25br
The Stockmarket International / Bill Stormont: p 22cl
Hideo Haga / Arcadia Photo: p 25tl; p 26br; p 34bl
Press Foto, Florence: p 30bl
The Stockmarket International / Ariel Skelley: p 35tr

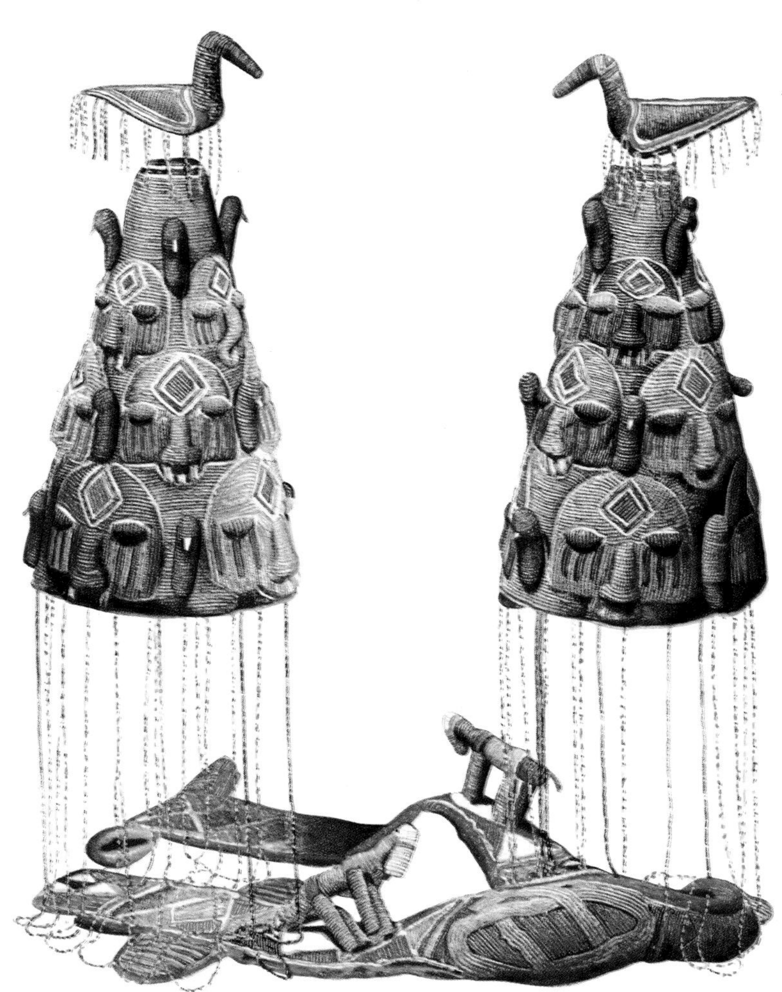